This Book Belongs To:

____

Wayfinders LITTLE BIOGRAPHIES OF HAWAI'I'S LEADERS

EDDIE AIKAU

LEGENDARY LIFEGUARD AND SURFER

written by David Del Rocco

illustrated by Storm Kano

BeachHouse

"Eddie Would Go!"

Everybody in Hawai'i knows this phrase.
But who was Eddie?

Edward Ryon Makuahanai Aikau was born May 4, 1946, on Maui. His family was descended from the high priests of King Kamehameha I and King Kamehameha II. Eddie first learned how to surf at Kahului Harbor. He loved the ocean and dreamed of being a great surfer like his hero, Duke Kahanamoku.

When he was fourteen, Eddie moved to Oʻahu with his parents, sister, and four brothers. The Aikau family settled in an unusual place: a Chinese cemetery near the slopes of Punchbowl. The area was full of mango, banana, and guava trees.

Although at first the Aikau children were a little scared about living in a graveyard, they got used to it and began to love their new home. They would play hide-and-seek at night among the tombstones.

Eddie was devoted to surfing. As a young man, he surfed the giant waves at Waimea Bay on O‘ahu’s North Shore. People once thought no one could ride the enormous waves there. Some of the waves that Eddie surfed were more than forty feet high!

Eddie was the first lifeguard at Waimea Bay. As a lifeguard, he saved over 500 people! He never lost one swimmer on his watch. In 1971 he was named "Lifeguard of the Year." He also met Linda Crosswhite, a tourist from Seattle who would become his wife.

Eddie competed in surfing events, and in 1977, he won the famous Duke Kahanamoku Invitational Surfing Contest. He was proud of his Hawaiian heritage. When he won, he said, "I did it for all the Hawaiians!"

Eddie and his brothers were also talented musicians. They played music and sang at all of their family lūʻau. The Aikau family showed Linda true Hawaiian hospitality and the aloha spirit. And although she returned to Seattle, she came back to Hawaiʻi and married Eddie the next year.

In 1978, the Polynesian Voyaging Society gathered a crew to sail a traditional Polynesian voyaging canoe from Hawai'i to Tahiti. The canoe was named the *Hōkūle'a* (Star of Gladness).

Although they had made a successful voyage to Tahiti in 1976, this would be the first one without an escort boat. For navigation, the crew would rely only on the stars and the signs of nature, like their ancestors did. Eddie was so excited to be chosen for this experience.

HOKULE'A

On March 16, the *Hōkūle'a* left O'ahu. Unfortunately, the weather was extremely bad. The waves were fierce. The canoe started taking on water, and the wind and waves flipped the canoe over. All the crew members had to hang on for their lives. They had no way to call for help.

After many hours, Eddie volunteered to paddle his surfboard to the island of Lāna'i to get help. This was a very scary, courageous, and selfless decision. Eddie tied some oranges around his neck and set out. A few minutes after he left, his life jacket came floating back to the canoe. The crew realized he must have taken it off so that he could paddle faster.

When the crew was finally rescued, the state of Hawai'i began the largest ever air-and-sea search to look for Eddie. Sadly, Eddie was never seen again. Because of his bravery and his willingness to make such a daring swim to save his friends, Eddie will always be remembered as a hero.

Eddie was a remarkable and caring person. He was famous, but he always remained quiet and humble.

In his honor, a surfing contest is held at Waimea Bay on the North Shore of O'ahu, where Eddie was a lifeguard. People call it "The Eddie," and the contest runs only when waves reach forty feet. It is open only to those surfers who can surf giant waves like Eddie did. These surfers come from around the world to honor Eddie's memory and his legacy of helping others.

Eddie's wife, Linda, shared that the phrase "Eddie would go" was first said by big wave surfer Mark Foo as he looked out at the huge waves breaking at Waimea Bay.

We will always remember Eddie for his kindness, his gentle nature, and his amazing bravery.

LIST OF SOURCES

Coleman, Stuart Holmes. *Eddie Would Go.* New York: St. Martin's Griffin Press, 2001.

"The Eddie Aikau Big Wave Invitational." https://www.theeddieaikau.com.

Hawaiian: The Legend of Eddie Aikau. Directed by Sam George. ESPN Films, 30 for 30 series. Bristol, CT: ESPN Films, 2013.

"The Surfing Life Story of Eddie Aikau." Surfer Today. https://www.surfertoday.com/surfing/the-surfing-life-story-of-eddie-aikau.

EDDIE AIKAU
FOUNDATION

The Eddie Aikau Foundation (EAF) nonprofit was formed in 2000 by the Aikau Family to honor Eddie's memory and his accomplishments as a courageous Honolulu City & County lifeguard and legendary big wave surfer. The foundation pays tribute to Eddie's passion for helping others. He was a true symbol of the aloha spirit, and they share his story to inspire young and old people alike to be productive members of their community, helping others whenever they can. The EAF conducts annual essay contests for seventh through tenth grade students throughout Hawai'i and published a bilingual children's book by Jonathan Ibanez, a student from Maui, in 2010. The EAF has managed the Eddie Big Wave Invitational surf contest and annual opening ceremony since 2017.

Visit www.eddieaikaufoundation.org and www.theeddieaikau.com to learn more and to donate so they may continue their work in the community.

About the Author

David Del Rocco is a retired high school teacher who lives and works in Honolulu. He has a BA in the Hawaiian Language from the University of Hawaiʻi, a BA in Spanish from Rutgers University, and an MLIS from the University of Hawaiʻi.

About the Illustrator

Storm Kano is a published illustrator of local children's books. Born and raised on Oʻahu, she hopes to give back to her community through the art of visual storytelling. When she's not drawing, Storm enjoys exploring the natural beauty of the island and cuddling with her dog, Toby. For more information, visit www.StormKano.art.

Wayfinders LITTLE BIOGRAPHIES OF HAWAIʻI'S LEADERS

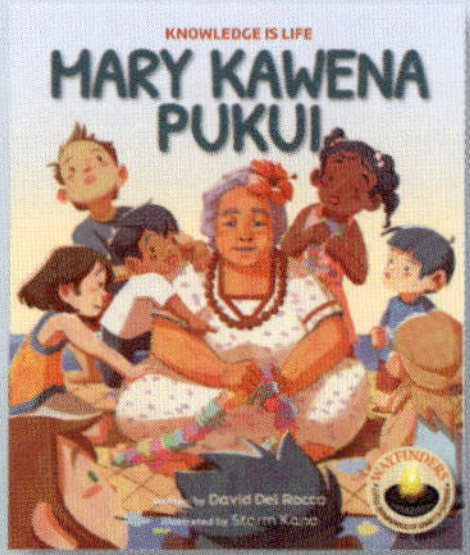

ISBN: 978-1-949000-38-2 • Library of Congress Control Number: 2025931711
Illustrations by Storm Kano • Design by Jane Gillespie
First Printing, June 2025

BeachHouse Publishing • PO Box 5464 • Kāneʻohe, Hawaiʻi 96744
info@beachhousepublishing.com • www.beachhousepublishing.com
Printed in China

EDDIE
WOULD
GO!